World of Insects

Fireflies

by Connie Colwell Miller

Consultant:
Gary A. Dunn, MS, Director of Education
Young Entomologists' Society Inc.
Lansing, Michigan

Capstone
press

Mankato, Minnesota

Bridgestone Books are published by Capstone Press,
151 Good Counsel Drive, P.O. Box 669, Mankato, Minnesota 56002.
www.capstonepress.com

Library of Congress Cataloging-in-Publication Data
Miller, Connie Colwell, 1976–
   Fireflies / by Connie Colwell Miller.
      p. cm.—(Bridgestone Books. World of insects)
   Includes bibliographical references and index.
   ISBN 0-7368-3707-8 (hardcover)
   1. Fireflies—Juvenile literature. I. Title. II. Series: World of insects.
QL596.L28M55 2005
595.76'44—dc22   2004013076

Summary: A brief introduction to fireflies, discussing their characteristics, habitat, life cycle, and
   predators. Includes a range map, life cycle illustration, and amazing facts.

Editorial Credits
Erika L. Shores, editor; Jennifer Bergstrom, designer; Erin Scott, Wylde Hare Creative, illustrator;
   Jo Miller, photo researcher; Scott Thoms, photo editor

Photo Credits
Ann & Rob Simpson, 10
Bill Beatty, 12
Brand X Pictures, back cover
Bruce Coleman Inc./Laura Riley, 4; Robert L. Dunne, 18
Dwight R. Kuhn, cover
Photo Researchers Inc./Science Photo Library/Darwin Dale, 20; Steve Percival, 16
Visuals Unlimited/Jeff Daly, 1, 6

1 2 3 4 5 6 10 09 08 07 06 05

Table of Contents

Fireflies

Have you ever seen an insect that glows in the dark? Fireflies are insects known for doing just that. They are often called lightningbugs because of their blinking glow.

Most fireflies make chemicals that cause part of their bodies to glow. Fireflies glow during both day and night. People usually see fireflies glowing only at night.

Fireflies are not flies. Flies have only one pair of wings. Like ladybugs, fireflies are beetles. They have two pairs of wings.

◄ Hundreds of fireflies light up the night.

6

What Fireflies Look Like

There are many kinds of fireflies, but all share some features. Fireflies have a hard outer covering that protects their bodies. This **exoskeleton** is usually brown or black.

Fireflies have three body sections. Their head has eyes and two **antennas**. Wings and six legs join to the middle section called the **thorax**. The **abdomen** is the end section. The abdomen of most fireflies glows.

◀ Fireflies use only one pair of wings to fly. The other wings protect the flying wings.

Firefly Range Map

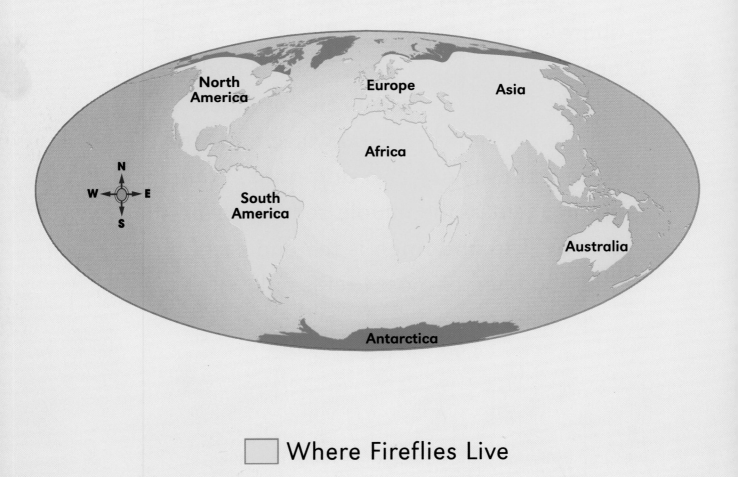

☐ Where Fireflies Live

Fireflies in the World

At least 2,000 types of fireflies live in the world. Fireflies can live everywhere except Arctic areas and Antarctica. Fireflies are most common in warm places. Many kinds of fireflies live in tropical Asia, Central America, and South America. In the United States, fireflies that glow are found only east of the Rocky Mountains.

◄ Fireflies live almost everywhere in the world.

Firefly Habitats

Most fireflies live in damp areas. They find homes in rotting wood or near streams and ponds. During the day, adult fireflies rest on leaves and branches. Firefly **larvae** live beneath rotting leaves and plants. They find their food there.

◀ Adult fireflies rest during the day.

What Fireflies Eat

Firefly larvae eat slugs, snails, and earthworms. They also eat the young of other insects.

Scientists think most adult fireflies eat nothing at all. Adult fireflies live only a short time. Much of this time is spent looking for mates. Some adult fireflies eat **nectar**. Insects get this liquid from plants.

◀ Firefly larvae eat slugs. Larvae must eat plenty of food to grow into adults.

Life Cycle of a Firefly

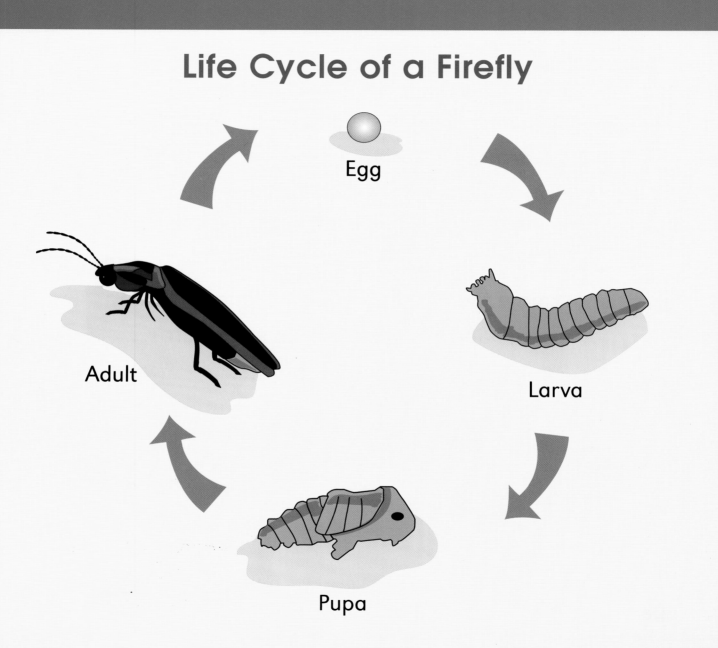

Egg

Larva

Pupa

Adult

Eggs and Larvae

To produce young, a female firefly mates with a male in summer. The female firefly then lays eggs in soil or on the bottoms of leaves. After about four weeks, larvae hatch from the eggs. Larvae look like small glowing worms. Some people call them glowworms.

Firefly larvae eat and grow all summer. In fall, they dig tunnels in the ground. The larvae live in the tunnels until spring.

Pupae and Adults

In spring, firefly larvae come out of the ground. They eat and grow.

Growing firefly larvae build blankets of soil. They crawl inside these blankets. Fireflies are called **pupae** while they are in the blankets. The pupae change inside the soil blankets. They develop their adult antennas and legs. About six weeks later, they become adult fireflies.

◄ Firefly larvae eat and grow before they become pupae.

Dangers to Fireflies

Fireflies have some **predators**. These animals eat fireflies. Firefly predators include frogs, spiders, birds, and other fireflies. Some female fireflies eat male fireflies.

Fireflies defend themselves against predators. To some animals, fireflies may taste bad. The firefly's blinking may warn predators not to eat them.

Fireflies have predators, but they are still plentiful. Perhaps you can spot fireflies glowing on warm summer nights.

◄ Some fireflies eat other fireflies.

Amazing Facts about Fireflies

- A male firefly flashes its light about every five seconds. A female flashes its light about every two seconds.
- People use fireflies in medical research. The firefly has two rare chemicals used in research on cancer and other diseases. Scientists can't make these chemicals on their own.
- Adult fireflies live only three to four months.
- Some kinds of fireflies live underwater.

← Unlike a lightbulb, a firefly's light gives off no heat.

Glossary

abdomen (AB-duh-muhn)—the end section of an insect's body

antenna (an-TEN-uh)—a feeler on an insect's head

exoskeleton (eks-oh-SKEL-uh-tuhn)—the hard outer covering of an insect

larva (LAR-vuh)—an insect at the stage after an egg; more than one larva are larvae.

nectar (NEK-tur)—a sweet liquid that some insects collect from flowers and eat as food

predator (PRED-uh-tur)—an animal that hunts other animals for food

pupa (PYOO-puh)—an insect at the stage of development between a larva and an adult; more than one pupa are pupae.

thorax (THOR-aks)—the middle section of an insect's body; wings and legs are attached to the thorax.

Read More

Jacobs, Liza. *Fireflies.* Wild Wild World. San Diego: Blackbirch Press, 2003.

Walker, Sally M. *Fireflies.* Early Bird Nature Books. Minneapolis: Lerner, 2001.

Internet Sites

FactHound offers a safe, fun way to find Internet sites related to this book. All of the sites on FactHound have been researched by our staff.

Here's how:
1. Visit *www.facthound.com*
2. Type in this special code **0736837078** for age-appropriate sites. Or enter a search word related to this book for a more general search.
3. Click on the **Fetch It** button.

FactHound will fetch the best sites for you!

Index